GEOTHERMAL ENERGY
Hot Stuff!

Amy S. Hansen

PowerKiDS press.

New York

Powering Our World™

To Gail and David

Published in 2010 by The Rosen Publishing Group, Inc.
29 East 21st Street, New York, NY 10010

First Edition

Editor: Amelie von Zumbusch
Book Design: Greg Tucker
Photo Researcher: Jessica Gerweck

Photo Credits: Cover Arctic-Images/Getty Images; pp. 5, 7, 11, 17, 22 Shutterstock.com; p. 9 © Miguel Angel Munoz/age fotostock; pp. 13, 19 © Kim Steele/Getty Images; p. 17 (inset) © Biosphoto/Boulton Mark/Peter Arnold, Inc.; p. 21 Robert Glenn/Getty Images.

Library of Congress Cataloging-in-Publication Data

Hansen, Amy
  Geothermal energy: hot stuff! / Amy S. Hansen.
      p. cm. — (Powering our world)
  Includes index.
  ISBN 978-1-4358-9330-6 (library binding) — ISBN 978-1-4358-9748-9 (pbk.) — ISBN 978-1-4358-9749-6 (6-pack)
  1. Geothermal resources—Juvenile literature. I. Title.
  GB1199.5.H36 2010
  621.44—dc22
                                2009026098

Manufactured in the United States of America
CPSIA Compliance Information: Batch #113160PK: For Further Information Contact Rosen Publishing, New York, New York at 1-800-237-9932

Contents

Every fall, black ants move their nests deeper under ground. They do this to keep from **freezing**. It is warmer deeper under ground, thanks to Earth's geothermal energy. Geothermal energy is heat from inside Earth. If you go about 10 feet (3 m) down, the ground stays between 50 and 60° F (10–16° C). If you dug even deeper, you would find the **temperature** getting warmer and warmer.

People use geothermal energy to heat or cool buildings and to make electricity. Geothermal energy is a clean energy **source**. We do not pollute when we use it. Geothermal energy is also renewable. That means we cannot use it up.

You can see the hot steam escaping from Earth in this geothermal field. Geothermal fields are places where geothermal energy is easiest to capture.

Our Earth has three **layers**. They are the crust, mantle, and core. The core is at Earth's center. This is the hottest layer. It is still hot from when Earth formed, over four billion years ago. Much of Earth's heat is **generated** in the core and flows out to the mantle, Earth's middle layer.

The mantle has melted rocks, called magma. Magma heats up water deep under ground. When water reaches Earth's crust, or outside layer, it causes hot springs and **geysers**. It also powers geothermal energy systems. Earth's crust is warmed by the Sun. We use energy from the crust for geothermal energy systems called geothermal heat pumps.

Yellowstone National Park's Castle Geyser, in Wyoming, often shoots water 90 feet (27 m) up into the air.

Geysers at Yellowstone National Park shoot hot water into the air. Long before there was a park, early Native Americans used these geysers. They cooked food and bathed in the hot water. Other ancient people used hot springs and geysers, too. The ancient Chinese and Japanese built baths around hot springs. The ancient Romans piped hot water out of hot springs and into their bathtubs.

In 1904, Italians went beyond what their Roman **ancestors** had done. They created the first geothermal power plant. The plant used steam that rose out of holes in the ground to make electricity.

The Romans built baths around hot springs in Bath, England, in the second century. Over 1,500 years later, the baths were rediscovered and rebuilt.

9

If you live near a hot spring, it is not hard to come up with uses for the hot water. For example, the people of Reykjavík, Iceland, use their hot springs to heat buildings. They pipe hot water from under ground through their buildings.

Geothermal energy can also help plants grow. Farmers build **greenhouses** that use geothermal energy in some places where farming is hard. Inside the greenhouses, there are pipes full of hot water drawn up from under ground. The hot water warms both the soil and the air inside the building. People use this method to grow vegetables in Hungary, Italy, Iceland, and New Mexico.

Many buildings in Boise, Idaho, are heated by geothermal energy, including the state capitol and more than half of the businesses downtown.

Most kinds of power plants use energy to heat water and create steam. The steam rises and turns **turbines**, which make electricity. This is easy with geothermal power plants since most of them start out with hot water.

There are several kinds of geothermal plants. In flash steam plants, **engineers** pipe hot, **pressurized** water from under ground to the surface. When they lower the pressure, the water turns to steam, or flashes. In binary power plants, engineers use hot water to boil a liquid that creates steam to turn turbines.

The Geysers geothermal plants, in Santa Rosa, California, are dry steam plants. This means that they run on steam that rises out of the ground.

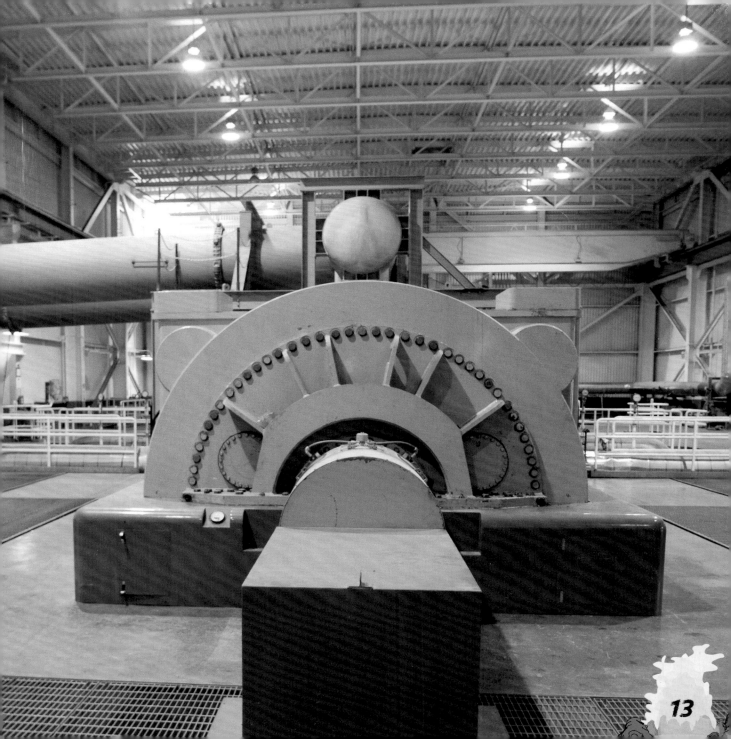

There are places where there is underground heat but no nearby water. Engineers are finding ways to bring water to these hot spots. Then we will be able to use the geothermal energy there.

Hot dry rock, or HDR, systems are one way to do this. Scientists in Los Alamos, New Mexico, began building the first HDR system in 1970. The system used three wells, each about 2 miles (3 km) deep. Engineers sent cold water down the first well. The cold water hit the hot rocks and broke them. The water turned hot. Some of it turned to steam. The steam and water then rose up through the other wells and turned turbines.

This drawing shows a hot dry rock system that uses a heat exchanger. There, hot water warms a liquid that is used to generate electricity.

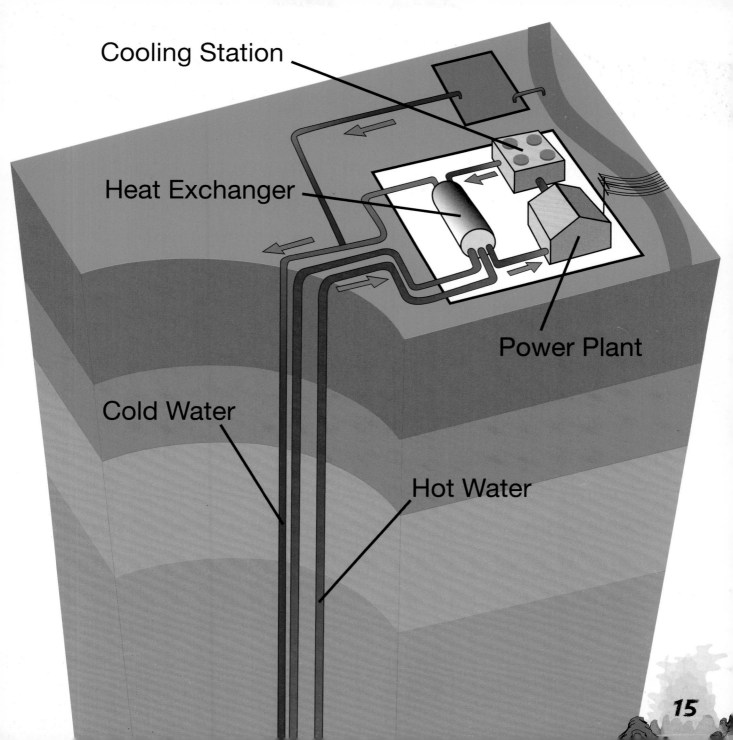

Cooling Station

Heat Exchanger

Power Plant

Cold Water

Hot Water

Heat for Your House

Engineers have also found ways to heat buildings with heat from Earth's crust when there is no water source. They use a heat pump to capture geothermal energy.

A heat pump starts by moving water through the ground. The water warms up. The warm water heats a gas called Freon. Next, the hot Freon enters a machine called a compressor. The compressor presses the gas into a smaller area. This makes the gas even hotter. A fan blows air over the hot Freon. The air warms up and is used to heat the building. In time, the compressor lets the Freon out. The gas cools it off, and the **cycle** starts again.

Geothermal heat pumps can keep buildings warm, even in the snowiest winters. *Inset:* Heat pumps are small enough to fit in most basements.

One of the biggest problems with geothermal power plants is that not everyone can use them. Geothermal power plants make clean energy, but they have to be built near a source of geothermal heat. In North America, most of those sources are in the West.

A second problem is that engineers find that some geothermal power plants run out of steam. They are fixing this problem by adding more water. For example, the city of Santa Rosa, California, pipes its cleaned wastewater to a group of geothermal plants called The Geysers. The water keeps the power plants working.

The Geysers, seen here, produce enough energy for 725,000 homes.
Inset: The dark spots on this map are the best spots for geothermal energy.

Geothermal energy use is becoming more and more common. Some new schools use geothermal heat pumps instead of **furnaces** or air conditioners. Farmers can keep fish in ponds warmed by geothermal heat. Running pipes of warm water under sidewalks can keep them clear of snow.

Engineers are now looking for ways to get more energy from Earth. They are experimenting with drilling deeper to collect more heat. They are finding places where magma can be easily reached. In 2007, 24 countries used geothermal heat to make electricity. Today, that number is growing!

Geothermal energy is used to produce the electricity needed to run many household machines, such as washing machines and clothes dryers.

Geothermal Energy Timeline

4 billion years ago	Earth forms as a fiery ball. It begins to cool off slowly.
10,000 years ago	Early Native Americans cook and bathe in the geysers in what is now Yellowstone National Park.
79 CE	Mount Vesuvius **erupts**. It destroys the geothermal-heated Roman baths in Pompeii, Italy.
1892	Engineers in Boise, Idaho, use hot springs to heat local buildings.
1904	Engineers in Lardello, Italy, make electricity with the first geothermal power generator.
1948	Carl Nielsen builds the first geothermal heat pump in his home in Ohio.
1960	Pacific Gas and Electric starts the first large dry steam power plant in the United States, at The Geysers, in California.
1974	Engineers in Los Alamos, New Mexico, start working with hot dry rock electricity systems.
1980	Brawley, California, becomes home to the first flash power plant in the United States.
1981	The first binary geothermal power plant begins producing energy in Raft River, Idaho.

ancestors (AN-ses-terz) Relatives who lived long ago.

cycle (SY-kul) Actions that happen in the same order over and over.

engineers (en-juh-NEERZ) Masters at planning and building engines, machines, roads, and bridges.

erupts (ih-RUPTS) Breaks open.

freezing (FREEZ-ing) Becoming cold enough to turn to ice.

furnaces (FUR-nes-ez) Things in which heat is produced.

generated (JEH-nuh-rayt-ed) Made.

geysers (GY-zerz) Springs that send up a jet of hot water or steam.

greenhouses (GREEN-hows-ez) Buildings that trap heat to make it warm enough to grow plants.

layers (LAY-erz) Thicknesses of something.

pressurized (PREH-shuh-ryzed) Under a force that pushes things together.

source (SORS) The place from which something starts.

temperature (TEM-pur-cher) How hot or cold something is.

turbines (TER-bynz) Motors that turn by a flow of water or air.

Index

Web Sites

Due to the changing nature of Internet links, PowerKids Press has developed an online list of Web sites related to the subject of this book. This site is updated regularly. Please use this link to access the list:
www.powerkidslinks.com/pow/geo/